SHARK'S TEETH
Nose Art

Jeffrey L. Ethell

Airlife
England

This edition first published in 1992 by Airlife Publishing, Ltd., Shrewsbury, England

©Jeffrey L. Ethell, 1992

ISBN 1 85310 380 2

Published by Motorbooks International, P.O. Box 2, 729 Prospect Avenue, Osceola, WI 54020, USA, 1992

Printed and bound in Hong Kong

Airlife Publishing Ltd.
101 Longden Road, Shrewsbury, England

On the front cover: Though the Flying Tigers made shark's teeth famous, creating an avalanche of copies, it was No. 112 Squadron, Royal Air Force (RAF), which first put the fierce mouth on a Curtiss P-40, an ideal mechanical shape for the artwork. Here No. 112's commander, Squadron Leader P.F. Illingworth, poses in the western desert with the Kittyhawk he flew from July 1943 to March 1944. *Frank F. Smith*

On the back cover: Top, a US Army T-34C Turbo Mentor at Pope Air Force Base, North Carolina. *Douglas A. Zalud* Bottom, a No. 475 Squadron, Royal Australian Air Force Spitfire over Morotai in June 1945. *Frank F. Smith.*

On the frontispiece: A 23rd Tactical Fighter Wing A-10 Thunderbolt II. The 23rd Wing is a direct descendant of the World War II 23rd Fighter Group, which absorbed the American Volunteer Group when it disbanded on July 4, 1942. The shark's teeth on their aircraft are proud reminders of the unit's lineage. *Douglas A. Zalud*

On the title page: When the VF-111 Sundowners were equipped with Phantoms they quickly transferred their shark's teeth, which had become an accepted part of the squadron's markings in spite of Navy regulations. This was their 1976 Bicentennial paint scheme when flying off the USS *Coral Sea*. *Larry Davis*

Contents

Introduction

Aircraft nose art has been a part of aviation ever since there was enough fabric on the side of a fuselage to serve as a canvas. From the beginnings of recorded history humans have felt a need to personalize weapons of war with individual heraldry. There is no better example of this than art which made the weapon seem even more fierce. The raging animal face has been a favorite, particularly one with sharp teeth ready to gobble up the enemy.

When the airplane emerged as a weapon of war, crews began transferring fierce faces to their machines, even when there was very little nose on which to paint. When the streamlined Roland C.II entered German service in 1915 its shape led to the name *Walfisch* (Whale). Before long, through the impetus of pilots such as Oberleutnant Ritter von Schleich, mouths and eyes were painted on the front of the Rolands to match the name, and within a short time the markings evolved into a genuine shark mouth.

By mid-war the shark face with its jagged teeth and cold-blooded eyes was glaring across both sides, painted on bombers, fighters, observation aircraft, and even the most nonthreatening of warplanes. German pilots were given complete freedom to paint individual markings on their front-line aircraft, whereas the British were limited, generally, to painting training aircraft that were kept out of harm's way.

According to World War I aviation historian Greg VanWyngarden, "The idea for 'facial' markings on the noses of airplanes was arrived at in different units and air forces totally independent of each other. The large 'open-mouthed' cowlings of rotary-engined aircraft invited comparisons with mouths rather obviously . . . for example French Nieuports with mouths and eyes on their cowlings. A contemporary German writer, M. E. Kahnert, wrote in his book *Jagdstaffel 356* (a fictionalized account of a German fighter squadron, but fairly authentic) about Sopwith Camels: 'Their rotary engines look like huge fish-mouths.'

"Furthermore, the big bulbous noses of Allied pushers, such as the Belgian Farmans, or twin-engined German bombers, like the AEG G.IV and Friedrichshafen G.II, were open invitations for the application of facial markings."

By the time America entered the war there was a pattern to follow. The 9th Aero Squadron, the first American night reconnaissance squadron in combat, painted the Breguet 14s of its 1st Flight black with massive teeth on the nose. The bizarre impression was of a fish, a whale or a night-flying insect, and the tail of one seemed to carry painted scales, completing the impression of a flying fish.

American 1st Lt. Ralph A. O'Neill, 147th Aero Squadron, painted his Nieuport 28 as a direct reaction to his encounters with garish German fighters. "The German aces, particularly Richthofen's Flying Circus . . . , had painted their planes in a horrible way, with skulls and crossbones and hideous colors, to intimidate the Allied fliers. I painted my plane [as] a shark with a great gaping mouth [and] large teeth." O'Neill had been through training at Issoudun where Capt. Harry S. Gwinne's Nieuport was painted with a shark mouth and massive scales across the fuselage—this may have been the inspiration. Certainly by 1918 the motif was established. With the end of hostilities it was not unusual to find the rapacious grin on most airfields. The tradition has remained popular with aircrews to the present day.

Between the wars, declining military budgets meant that, by sheer decreases in the number of aircraft, fewer examples of nose art would show up, including the shark mouth. Nevertheless, a few hearty souls kept the tradition alive, even on civilian aircraft.

Just before the German invasion of Poland in September 1939 and the start of World War II, the shark mouth was back on German airplanes. The Luftwaffe's 2./JG 71 Messerschmitt Bf 109Cs and 2./StG 77 Junkers Ju 87Bs had shark's teeth on their angular snouts before they went to war. Once the fighting started, the hungry shark was copied by others.

The first unit known by its shark mouths was II./ZG 76, nicknamed the Haifisch Gruppe, or Shark Group, in April 1941. Its Messerschmitt 110s looked spectacular—certainly more so than the aircraft itself, which proved to be easy prey for single-engine fighters.

When No. 112 Squadron Royal Air Force (RAF) encountered ZG 76 over Greece and Crete in its Gladiator biplanes, the Bf 110 was lethal by comparison, well suited to its shark namesake. After No. 112 was transferred to Egypt and reequipped with the Curtiss Tomahawk, an export version of the P-40, the idea surfaced of painting shark mouths on the fighters. Though inspired to a degree by ZG 76, the mouth took on a different style, one suited almost perfectly for the Tomahawk's shape. Though no one foresaw it, this led to the P-40 becoming associated forever with shark's teeth. In the end the fighter lost much of its identity to the voracious visage on its nose.

The London *Illustrated News* did a piece on the Tomahawks of 112 Squadron that reached around the globe and settled in Burma. On 15 November 1941 ten pilots of the American Volunteer Group (AVG) were having dinner at the Baptist mission in Rangoon, Burma, after getting their initial cockpit checks in the AVG's Tomahawks. Both Erik Shilling and Charley Bond saw a No. 112 Tomahawk on the cover of the recently arrived *News* section. Shilling had seen photos of ZG 76's 110s so the idea wasn't new, but everyone was taken with how powerful an image the shark mouth projected when on the P-40.

The pilots became pretty excited about using the mouth as a squadron marking, but when the idea was put before Claire Chennault he wanted it used as a group insignia on the P-40s of all three AVG squadrons. Within a few days most of the pilots were busy chalking the teeth onto their fighters so either they or local artists could paint them on. As a result, almost every shark mouth in the AVG was unique, though the basic 112 Squadron pattern was followed.

Shilling was adamant about the art retaining the cold, expressionless, staring impression of the real shark who "didn't give a damn who he hit, he was just out to get someone." On November 17, 1941, AVG pilot R. T. Smith recorded in his diary, "Didn't fly any today but got started painting up my ship [No. 77]. We are making shark-heads out of the front end.

Looks mean as hell." Crew chief Mel Kemph recalled that several of the mouths were painted by Chinese artists who were real pros with a wonderful eye for mixing colors. Charley Bond wrote in his diary on November 19, "I stayed busy by helping Ed Rector paint the tiger shark on the nose of his plane."

Just over a month later, after their first combats with the Japanese, the AVG found the press had given them a new label, one that would make them famous: the Flying Tigers.

Though other combat units in World War II would find their own versions of the shark mouth, the Flying Tigers were splashed across headlines and through magazines. Their airborne teeth inspired countless copies, particularly on the P-40s of the 23rd Fighter Group, the US Army Air Forces unit that absorbed the AVG on July 4, 1942. Lt. Col. "Jack" Chennault, son of the AVG's founder, painted tiger faces on the P-40Es of his 11th Fighter Squadron in the Aleutian Islands.

The 25th Squadron of the 51st Fighter Group at Assam, India, came up with a clever variation on the theme. As ground crewman Homer G. Cozby recalled, "A young pilot of our squadron, a Lieutenant McClung, was a former employee of Walt Disney Studios. Out of the mysterious legends of the Far East, artist McClung came up with the squadron emblem or motif, the semi-famous Assam Draggin'. Some ways similar to the existing tiger-shark mouth on the P-40s in China, yet awesomely different with long, sabre-like tusks out of an open mouth filled with pointed teeth, its red eyes glared ferociously at any air or ground target. . . . I painted many, many Assam Draggin' mouths on our squadron's planes."

As the war progressed almost every type of combat aircraft had shark's teeth painted on them, and some units and their aircraft were famous for their gaping mouths.

World War II was the heyday of the shark mouth, but there will never be a complete list of units which

painted them on their aircraft.

Though units were disbanded and reinstated throughout the postwar era, the shark mouth managed to reappear with both No. 112 Squadron's Vampires, Sabres, and Hunters and the 51st Fighter Group's F-86 Sabres. During the Korean War the 12th Fighter Bomber Squadron's F-51 Mustangs were decorated with large shark's teeth, as were numerous other aircraft.

With a few exceptions, nose art in general faded during the 1950s and early 1960s but with another war, this time in Vietnam, and the relaxed rules in combat theaters, personal markings came back. As F-105s headed up into North Vietnam, shark mouths reappeared. When the 388th Tactical Fighter Wing received its new F-4Es, the gaping mouths seemed ideally suited for this gun-equipped version of the Phantom II. The brass were not pleased with this resurgence, and the teeth were ordered painted off.

In the post-Vietnam era shark's teeth resurfaced every now and then. The Wild Weasel F-105Gs of the 35th Tactical Fighter Wing and the Flying Tiger A-7s and A-10s of the 23rd Tactical Fighter Wing managed to keep their shark mouths but on the whole the marking reverted to an individual decoration.

During the late 1980s nose art, particularly in the US Air Force, came back into official favor. The shark mouth had become a military icon and it was painted back onto new-generation aircraft with gusto. The floodgates opened in 1991 with Operation Desert Storm. Not only did the teeth get painted on numerous aircraft, particularly the A-10 and Tornado, but nose art was applied with near reckless daring.

Though official approval of shark's teeth on aircraft comes and goes, in the minds of military crews the marking has become a permanent part of their heritage and esprit de corps. No doubt little time will pass before one finds its way onto something like a space shuttle.

World War I To 1939

The skull and crossbones predated shark's teeth long before the invention of the airplane. The symbol of pirates and death, the Jolly Roger began to appear on military aircraft almost as soon as World War I had started. These German pilots and civilians seem quite happy to pose with it as painted on the spinner of an Albatros D.V. Norm Burtt via Greg VanWyngarden

A Roland C.II of Kampfstaffel 36 with shark's teeth. The aircraft was destroyed during a storm on the night of 29–30 August 1916. The mouth would later be enlarged until it took on the classic shape which would later show up in World War II. Greg VanWyngarden

One of the first pilots to paint a mouth on his aircraft was Oberleutnant Ritter von Schleich, shown here with his Roland C.II Walfisch (Whale) of Feldflieger Abteilung 2b, in late 1916 or early 1917. As with several Rolands, there is a pilot fish on the airspeed indicator strut. This whale face eventually evolved into a shark mouth on other C.IIs. Joseph Nieto via Peter M. Bowers

Capt. Fernand Jacquet and his observer, Lt. Henri Vindvoghel, stand in front of their Farman F.40, an ungainly and vulnerable pusher reconnaissance aircraft. Flying with 7e Escadrille Belge, the two became the first Belgians to shoot down an enemy plane, an Aviatik, on 17 April 1915. Considering the slow Farman a fighter, the two men would fly out to sea over the northern coastal front until far behind German lines, then head inland and ambush enemy aircraft. Jacquet was officially credited with seven kills though he was thought to have downed more. Peter M. Bowers

The crews of these L.V.G. C.IV reconnaissance two-seaters clearly felt the need to add some teeth to their usually nonthreatening machines. Though the observer had a rear-firing gun at his disposal, it took some excellent flying to avoid the more nimble single-seat Allied fighters. Don Malko

A Gotha G.III of Kagohl 2, spring 1917, possibly at Metz-Frescaty. Used only on the Western Front, this large bomber would harass Allied positions up and down the lines. Don Malko

A formation of Keystone LB-5A bombers flies up the coast in 1927. The aircraft had a top speed of 107mph and were a part of the Army's early strategic bombing force which was formed as a result of public reaction to Billy Mitchell's court martial in 1925. The fierce face on the bombers belied their vulnerability and 2,300lb payload of bombs. Charles W. Meyers via Joe Christy

Some aircraft were ideally suited for shark's teeth due to their unconventional configuration. When an engine could be mounted behind, leaving the nose clear for artwork, the results could be close to bizarre. David Ostrowski

MdL Georges Flachaire with his SPAD VII, Escadrille Spa 67. The eyes painted on the camshaft fairings were an obvious touch for the aircraft but very few were painted in this manner. Another of Flachaire's SPADs had teeth or tiger stripes added all the way around the cowling. Jon Guttman

When the Swiss Air Force bought its Messerschmitt 109s the aircraft seemed ideal for a set of teeth and some large glaring eyes. Peter Petrick

World War II, The Fighters

With the outbreak of World War II shark's teeth began to sprout on a number of different aircraft, but the first major appearance was on the Messerschmitt 110s of II Gruppe, ZG 76, the Haifisch (Shark) Gruppe. Peter Petrick

The teeth of ZG 76 took on a number of different forms. This 110 has more teeth than most of its stablemates. Matthiesen via Peter Petrick

A pilot of II Gruppe, ZG 76, climbs into his Bf 110, 1940. This style of shark mouth seemed to be the standard for the unit. Peter Petrick

Though this Bf 110 was not assigned to ZG 76, its shark mouth is fashioned more like the fish itself with detailed lips and blood dripping from its last meal. Peter Petrick

Several Gotha Go 242A combat gliders were painted with shark's teeth once in their operational theaters. Peter M. Bowers

Air defense P-38 Lightnings scramble from Glendale, California, just after the Pearl Harbor attack, 1941. Though the Japanese invasion never materialized, submarine patrols and pilots standing alert were common on the West Coast.

The 39th Fighter Squadron P-38F of Curran L. "Jack" Jones at Milne Bay, New Guinea, in late 1942. The P-38's engine nacelles were ideally suited for shark's teeth and the eyes fit perfectly around the small exhaust manifold air scoops just behind the spinner. Norbert C. Ruff

Lt. Herbert Hasenfus climbs into his 54th Fighter Squadron P-38E in the Aleutians, 1942. USAF

15

Shark II *was F-5E Lightning No. 698 attached to the 12th Photo Recon Squadron, 3rd Photo Group, Twelfth Air Force at Florence, Italy, in November 1944. The noses were red and white with the names* Boots *on the right side of the nose and* Vera *on the right engine nacelle.* Ralph P. Willett

An F-5 Lightning of the 7th Photo Group, Eighth Air Force, at Mount Farm, England, in 1944. John and Donna Campbell

A P-39D Airacobra of the 80th Fighter Squadron, 8th Fighter Group, New Guinea, in 1942. Though the shark mouth looked fierce, the Bell fighter was outclassed by Japanese fighters on almost all counts.

Lt. Norbert C. Ruff climbs into his 80th Fighter Squadron P-400 Airacobra at Twelve-Mile Drome, Port Moresby, New Guinea, July 1942. The P-400 was the export version of the P-39 originally sold to Britain but taken back after the attack on Pearl Harbor. Norbert C. Ruff

Margie was a P-51A of the 76th Squadron, 23rd Fighter Group at Szechwan, China, in April 1944. The 23rd absorbed the American Volunteer Group in July 1942 and shark's teeth have been painted on all the unit's aircraft to the present day. Steve Blake

When No. 112 Squadron, Royal Air Force, gave up its Kittyhawks for Mustangs, the shark mouth was transferred onto the new aircraft to good effect. Frank F. Smith

The 51st Fighter Group carried its shark's teeth through World War II in style, as seen on this 16th Squadron P-51C in China, 17 July 1944. Though the bazooka rocket tubes were used in combat, pilots recalled that their loud whistle, much like the Green Hornet's car, was more impressive than their effectiveness. USAF

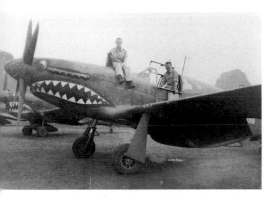

A P-51B Mustang of the 76th Squadron, 23rd Fighter Group, sits next to some of its P-40 shark mouth stablemates. Charlie Cook

Mouths on Mustangs in the European theater of operations (ETO) were a rarity. Maybe this incredible paint job around the time of the D-day invasion explains why.

Lt. Ian Mackenzie flew this shark into combat with the 402nd Squadron, 370th Fighter Group, ETO. Mackenzie via John and Donna Campbell

Jukin' Judy of the 422nd Night Fighter Squadron, Ninth Air Force, was flown by 1st Lt. E. Lee, with radar operator A. Dorner. Its crew chief was E. Jevyak. USAF/NASM

Lt. John R. Bennett flew the only shark-mouthed Mustang in the 352nd Fighter Group. Here Paul Grabb stands in front of the P-51B, coded HO-Y, serial number 43-6506. When Bennett received a P-51D replacement he painted a shark mouth on it as well. John L. Slabe via Sam Sox

The Spitfire VIIIs of No. 457 Squadron, Royal Australian Air Force, carried shark's teeth through the end of the war, flying out of Morotai with No. 80 Fighter Wing, No. 1 Tactical Air Force. The Name Grey Nurse *was painted on most of the squadron's aircraft.* Alfred Price

Lt. James H. Clark on the wing of his 382nd Squadron, 363rd Fighter Group, Mustang at Maupertus, France, with his crew (left to right) Stryzinski, Ellenberger, and Sikula. On 18 July 1944 Clark encountered a formation of Messerschmitt Bf 109s while flying The Mighty Midget; he shot down two and damaged two, for which he was later awarded the Silver Star. The inside of the mouth was red; the nose and trim on the mouth were yellow. Steve Blake

A close look at the shark mouth on a Spitfire VIII of No. 475 Squadron, Royal Australian Air Force. The teeth were dreamed up by Squadron Leader B. D. Watson as a tribute to No. 80 Wing Group Commanding Officer Capt. Clive R. Caldwell, who had commanded No. 112 Squadron with its shark-mouthed Tomahawks and Kittyhawks. Frank F. Smith

A No. 475 Squadron Spit VIII over Morotai in June 1945. Most of the fighters carried the No. 80 Wing ace of spades on the rudder. Frank F. Smith

P-40s Forever

Of all the aircraft which ever carried shark's teeth, the Curtiss P-40 is by far the most recognized. It all began with No. 112 Squadron, Royal Air Force, Tomahawks in the North African desert, 1941. This Kittyhawk was attached to 112 Squadron in 1942. Frank and Frieda Sanders/79th Fighter Group Association via John and Donna Campbell

Once the American Volunteer Group applied shark's teeth to their British lend-lease Tomahawks, the marking was forever enshrined in history as the Flying Tigers became famous. This flight of The 3rd Squadron, known as the Hell's Angels, steps up near the Burma-China border, 28 May 1942, during a patrol. R. T. Smith

No. 112 Squadron Kittyhawks running up in the western desert before a mission. Once the squadron's shark mouths became known, they served as patterns for countless aircraft across the globe in World War II, including Claire Chennault's Flying Tigers. Frank F. Smith

A No. 112 Squadron Warhawk carrying a bomb on the belly shackle, which could also hold an external fuel tank. Frank F. Smith

A group of Hell's Angels Squadron Flying Tigers during a refueling stop at Yunnanyi, China, 28 May 1943: standing (left to right) are Tommy Haywood and Arvid Olson, Jr.; sitting (left to right) are R. T. Smith, Ken Jernstedt, Bob Prescott, Link Laughlin, and Bill Reed. R. T. Smith

Tom Haywood flying an American Volunteer Group Tomahawk near the China-Burma border, May 1942. The shark mouths on each fighter were individually chalked in by their pilots, then painted. As a result no two were the same, though the general pattern was taken from No. 112 Squadron's markings in the western desert. R. T. Smith

American Volunteer Group ground crew refuel one of their Tomahawks in late 1941. NASM

Sgt. Bill Harris in the process of painting a shark mouth on a 75th Squadron, 23rd Fighter Group, P-40K at Hengyang, China. Harris painted the shark's teeth on squadron commander John Alison's Warhawk and on several other 75th Squadron aircraft. "I painted a lot of shark's mouths and eyes to look more vicious with longer tiger teeth in the front and an inverted eyebrow over the eye on some," said Harris. Bill Harris via Carl Molesworth

1st Lts. Edward J. Mulholland, Jr., and Donald J. Burch with Burch's P-40N Ruth-Less at Liangshan, China, in June or early July 1944. Both flew with the 7th Squadron, 3rd Fighter Group, Chinese-American Composite Wing. Note the Chinese national insignia under the wing. The aircraft also carried the number 665 on the fin and twelve alternating blue and white horizontal stripes on the rudder. Burch had one Japanese flag under the windshield for his kill of 9 March 1944. He would get another kill on 23 July, and Mulholland scored two kills before both were shot down in October 1944—Burch became a prisoner of war and Mulholland evaded capture to return in January 1945. Wilbur Walton via Carl Molesworth

1st Lt. Yoh Kung-Cheng with a P-40N of the 27th Squadron, 5th Fighter Group, Chinese-American Composite Wing (CACW). The 27th's insignia is painted above the exhaust stacks—the number 27 on a red lightning arrow with wings. The 27th was the last CACW squadron to fly P-40s and did not convert to P-51s until June 1945. The white spinner was the standard marking of the 5th Group, which was based at Chihkiang from late spring 1944 until the end of the war. Yoh (spelled Yueh in some references) was credited with three air-to-air victories. Santo Savoka via Carl Molesworth

The P-40 was such an ideal shape for all types of faces that variation became the rule. This parrot face, though not as fierce as a shark, took up quite a bit of room on the nose, as did the large skulls of the 80th Fighter Group based at Assam, India.

Packard-built Rolls-Royce Merlin-powered P-40Fs of the 68th Squadron, 317th Fighter Group, on patrol out of Guadalcanal, 1942. Rollins Snelling via Doug Canning

The 68th Fighter Squadron artist has his red and white paint cans out to touch up the shark mouth on this P-40F at Guadalcanal, 1942. Rollins Snelling via Doug Canning

A 25th Squadron, 51st Fighter Group, P-40N at Tingkawk, Burma, in 1944, loaded with bombs and external fuel just before a mission. Kenneth M. Sumney

When John "Jack" Chennault, son of the Flying Tigers' famous commander, led the 11th Squadron, 343rd Fighter Group, in the Aleutians, he emulated the shark mouth by painting tiger faces on some of the unit's P-40Es. National Archives

World War II, The Bombers

Numerous A-20s of the 312th Bomb Group, Fifth Air Force, had a skull and crossbones painted on the nose around the forward firing .50 caliber machine guns. Along with the B-25, the Havoc lived up to its name in destroying enemy shipping and strafing.

One of the early modified strafers in the Pacific, Hell's-Fire, a B-25D of the 500th Squadron, 345th Bomb Group, was transferred from the 3rd Bomb Group in November 1943. It was shot down on 2 September 1944 with 2nd Lt. Allan W. Lay at the controls. Several Mitchells of the 500th were painted with shark's teeth.

Barry's Baby was an A-20G of the 90th Squadron, 3rd Bomb Group, Fifth Air Force. The squadron's shark mouths became a trademark in the theater. Frank F. Smith

Runt's Roost was another early Mitchell strafer with .50 caliber guns fitted in the glass nose, which was painted over, and in side blister packs. Maj. Paul "Pappy" Gunn was a key figure in creating this devastating ground-attack package.

A B-25D strafer with the 499th Squadron, 345th Bomb Group of the Air Apaches. Lady Ruth *flew through the war and ended up being surplused as war weary.*

A 499th Squadron, 345th Bomb Group, B-25 at Clark Field, Philippines, June 1945. Head on, the unit's shark-mouthed bat insignia was an awesome sight, particularly if all the forward firing machine guns were winking. USAF/NASM

Below and below left
The "Bats Outa' Hell" nose art of the 499th Squadron, 345th Bomb Group, B-25s was very elaborate considering the unit artists tried to paint it on every bomber. The blue bat with red and white mouth and eyes was visible for quite a long way, even in the air. There were several variations on the theme but the basic configuration was always the same. Ernest McDowell

The 38th Bomb Group's B-25s had three squadrons of shark's teeth based on dragons, wolves, and tigers while flying in the southwest Pacific. The 405th Squadron was a series of Green Dragons, seen here in one form on this B-25J. NASM

The 71st Squadron of the 38th Bomb Group painted nose art to match their Wolfhead insignia. NASM

The 405th Bomb Squadron's Green Dragons were colorful to say the least—and certainly a job for any nose artist to paint onto an airplane in the middle of a combat theater as hostile and uncomfortable as the southwest Pacific. John Campbell and Dana Bell

This 823rd Squadron, 38th Bomb Group, Tiger, Kunai Kutter *was a cannon-carrying B-25G.*

A 405th Bomb Squadron B-25 revs up for takeoff. John Campbell via Dana Bell

Though the 340th Bomb Group, Twelfth Air Force, was not known for its shark's teeth, this 486th Squadron lead B-25J carries a well-rendered example on the way to attack targets in northern Italy, 3 January 1945. USAF

The 386th Bomb Group's A-26 Invaders carried quite a variety of faces, mouths and teeth with the Ninth Air Force over Europe. Carl Hildebrandt/Tim Bivens

Several B-26 Marauders of the 386th Bomb Group carried shark's teeth into action with the Ninth Air Force. NASM

The Marlin was one of the many 444th Squadron, 320th Bomb Group, B-26s which carried shark's teeth. The 444th was known for its grinning teeth and extremely well-rendered nose art, particularly Vargas pinup girls. USAF

Very few British bombers carried shark's teeth. This No. 419 Squadron, Royal Canadian Air Force, Lancaster B.X, VR-R, had all four cowlings painted with teeth. It flew sixty-three missions before the war was over. Al Davies via Clarence Simsonsen/Peter M. Bowers

Left and next page
Only a few B-17 Flying Fortresses had shark's teeth, such as these which flew with the Eighth Air Force. There was certainly plenty of nose area but it was normally used for pinups. Tiger Girl flew with the 388th Bomb Group, Latest Rumor with the 385th Group, and Flak Eater with the 305th Group.

Gremlin's Haven *was a B-24J of the 308th Bomb Group, Fourteenth Air Force, when the group was based near Kunming in early 1945. Bill Harris via Carl Molesworth*

Another 308th Bomb Group B-24, 80 Days was attached to the 374th Squadron as a replacement for an earlier B-24D of the same name.

The 320th Moby Dick Squadron of the 90th Bomb Group roamed across the Pacific with the Fifth Air Force carrying an impressive set of shark's teeth on most of its aircraft. The Jolly Rogers of the 90th were known for some of the most colorful nose art in the theater so the teeth fit in quite well. Lucky Stevens

Display of Arms *of the 320th Squadron, 90th Bomb Group, carried a pinup along with the squadron's smiling shark's teeth.* Frank F. Smith

90th Bomb Group B-24s on a mission in 1944. Note the skull and crossed bombs on the starboard tail fin. Frank F. Smith

Buzz-z Buggy *fit right in with the other shark mouths of the 308th Bomb Group, Fourteenth Air Force.*

The B-24 was an ideal subject for shark's teeth due to its massive, slab-sided nose. Rugged But Right, *an Eighth Air Force Liberator, had one of the most effective shark mouths painted on a bomber.* Mark H. Brown/USAFA

A 425th Squadron, 308th Bomb Group,
B-24L at Barrackpore, India, on 27
September 1945. Peter M. Bowers

When the 308th Bomb Group started
flying low-level, night sea-sweep missions
crews began to paint the bottom of their
aircraft black, which seemed to fit in very
well with the sinister nature of their
shark's teeth. Harry Friedman

Maulin' Mallard *of the 93rd Bomb Group, Eighth Air Force, had a total of 115 sorties recorded on the bomb behind Donald Duck.* Norm Taylor

One of the very few examples of teeth on a Canadian-based aircraft—this No. 10 Bomber Reconnaissance Squadron Liberator GR VI (a lend-lease B-24J) had a bright yellow tiger face, brown whiskers, eyebrows, and inner ear, black nose, mouth, and pupil, white teeth, blue irises and red lips, tongue, and blood drops. E. White via Peter M. Bowers

Liaison aircraft such as this Piper L-4 in Europe, 1944, were crucial to keeping ground commanders in touch during the push into Germany and for spotting artillery fire. Though they weren't known for their bite, their pilots were aggressive, even to the point of mounting bazooka rockets on their wing struts.

A liaison pilot, wearing the typical hard-working coveralls of a combat theater, stands next to his Piper L-4.

The hot rod of liaison grasshopper aircraft, this Stinson L-5 sits in a revetment of Tingkawk, Burma, in 1944. Peter M. Bowers

While shark-mouthed military aircraft got most of the attention, civilians emulated their more lethal brothers with some flattering copies, such as this 1940s era Luscombe which was used for research. NASM

With the release of thousands of wartime aircraft on the civil market, pilots found some very exotic types available. Dianna Bixby flew this Mosquito Mk. XXVI with shark's teeth on both the nose and the slipper external fuel tanks. Peter M. Bowers

Korea To Vietnam

With the end of World War II, shark's teeth, by sheer reduction in numbers of aircraft, faded from the scene, but there were exceptions. This Swiss Air Force P-51 Mustang of No. 21 Squadron was the only example of its type to carry teeth in Switzerland. Martin Kyburz

An F-51 in Korea. Don Spry

When the Korean War broke out in June 1950 the F-51 Mustang was put back into front-line service as a ground support aircraft. Though its liquid-cooled engine was vulnerable to ground fire, the Mustang did a tremendous job. The 12th Squadron, 18th Fighter Bomber Group, resurrected the shark mouth, flying out of Korean fields close to the fighting until their Mustangs were retired in favor of F-86s. Larry Davis via Merle Olmstead

A lineup of 12th Fighter Bomber Squadron Mustangs at Pusan, South Korea, in September 1950. US Air Force

The F-51 Vendetta *from the 12th Fighter Bomber Squadron.* Larry Davis via Merle Olmstead

Little Beast II *taxis out for a mission.* US Air Force

Little Beast II *being serviced on the flight line.* via Ernest McDowell

Not all nose art with teeth was painted to make the aircraft look like an animal. Apparently the pilot of this Korean War F-80C knew the reputation of twisters in the Midwest and had a creature painted to match it. USAF/NASM

Even bombs came in for treatment, though the art was gone in a single mission. The crewman on this F-84 Thunderjet has spent quite a bit of time on one of the fighter bomber's 500 lb bombs destined for a target in Korea. USAF/NASM

This F-80C Shooting Star of the 36th Squadron, 8th Fighter Bomber Wing, Suwon, fall 1952, went to war as The Beer City Special/Miss 33 II. *Bob Esposito*

Many F-86 Sabres of the 51st Fighter Interceptor Wing were painted with shark's teeth, with one of the flights in the 25th Squadron known as Tiger Flight.

This 51st Fighter Interceptor Wing F-86 Sabre was known as The Devilish Angel.

Korean War ten-victory ace Harold Fischer (left) and his crew chief, B. A. Sims, in front of their Sabre, The Paper Tiger. *The name was taken from Edgar Snow's book* Red Star Over China *in which the Chinese referred to Americans as paper tigers.* Harold Fischer

This US Air Force Air Defense Command T-33, Jaws, *served as a practice target for more modern fighters during air intercept practice. It had more than painted teeth— note the practice Sidewinder hung under the wing.* Norm Taylor

As the jet age gathered steam, the sleek noses of the new generation of aircraft provided excellent platforms for teeth, as seen on this Mexican Air Force No. 200 Squadron de Havilland Vampire F.Mk.3. Ismael Garcia Ilaca via Waechter/Dan Hagedorn

A B-26 Invader of the North Carolina Air National Guard in the 1950s. Alain Pelletier

The Dominican Republic's P-51s were all painted with shark's teeth. Lennart Engerby via Leif Hellstrom/Dan Hagedorn

When the Dominican Republic began to buy P-51 Mustangs, particularly from Sweden, it became one of the largest users of the aircraft in the postwar era. At one point, all of the fighters were painted with shark's teeth and different colors surrounding the mouths to designate different flights and squadrons. The result was some of the most colorful shark mouth nose art in history. Lennart Engerby via Leif Hellstrom/Dan Hagedorn

The Cavalier Aircraft Corporation rebuilt dozens of Mustangs for the US government's Military Assistance Program, which exported the fighters to Latin American nations. These Bolivian Air Force F-51s carry the stylized shark mouth of the Fuerza Aerea Boliviana and the tall Cavalier tails associated with many of the rebuilt aircraft. USAF

A Swiss Air Force Morane-Saulnier MS 406 in 1956, which was painted with shark's teeth when the last training course of Swiss pilots to use the aircraft came through. Since the old fighters were going to be scrapped, the Swiss Air Force allowed its young trainee pilots to paint them as they wished. Hans-Heiri Stapfer

A line of sharks . . . T-33s of the Ecuadorian Air Force. Though the "T-Bird" was primarily an advanced jet trainer, it could be fitted with guns and used in combat. Carlos Planas via Dan Hagedorn

This T-28A of the Mexican Air Force, though a trainer, looks just a bit more fierce with teeth. Bob Hanes via Dan Hagedorn

The intakes of the F-80 provided an ideal mouth for teeth, as seen on this Shooting Star of the Georgia Air National Guard. Bob Esposito

This Boeing B-47B at Wichita was assigned to the 306th Bomb Wing, MacDill Air Force Base, Florida, in 1952. John and Donna Campbell

A unique use of shark's teeth for an F-86D of the Oklahoma Air National Guard, Oklahoma City—paint them on the intake plug, which makes the aircraft look as if it has real teeth. John and Donna Campbell

A 61st Fighter Interceptor Squadron F-94B at Selfridge Air Force Base, Michigan, in 1955. Bob Stuckey via Jim Sullivan

F-86Ds of the 520th Squadron, 408th Fighter Interceptor Wing, Klamath Falls, Oregon, were painted with bright blue tails and an excellent variety of shark's teeth. John and Donna Campbell

Though the F-86D "Sabre Dog" was not greatly loved by its pilots, it served as an interceptor for many years before being passed on to the Air National Guard (ANG). This one flew with the Pennsylvania ANG. John and Donna Campbell

Letzter Vogel—*the last RF-84F in the German Air Force was painted as some garish bird of prey before it was decommissioned.* Larry Davis

An F-89D Scorpion of the 61st Fighter Interceptor Squadron at Harmon Field, 1956. Kitz via Larry Davis

This F-102A Delta Dagger flew with the Idaho Air National Guard. Alain Pelletier

Though US Navy regulations have always forbidden nose art on aircraft, it has popped up through the years. Apparently only one VMA-223 F9F-5 Panther on the line at Naval Air Station Whidbey Island in August 1955 could get away with having teeth. National Archives via Jim Sullivan

This F11F-1 Tiger of VF-21, 1956, shows the unit's shark's teeth. The squadron was one of the very few allowed to use such a marking on all of its aircraft. USN via David Ostrowski

Another VF-21 F11F at Naval Air Station Oceana, Virginia, with two instructor pilots, 17 November 1958. The squadron carried its shark mouths through the late 1950s. The tradition has survived through the F-4 era and into the current F-14 era. Peter B. Mersky

This China Lake QF-9G Cougar drone, 16 March 1967, survived seventeen test shots. Note the stenciled SNAFU 1 on the nose.
Clay Janson via Jim Sullivan

An F-8H Crusader of VF-111, with the "Double Nuts" modex number on the nose, at Naval Air Station Miramar on 19 March 1970. The Sundowners have carried a long tradition of shark's teeth all the way to the present day. Douglas D. Olson

This OV-10A of VAL-4, the Black Ponies, 1969, carried teeth on the drop tank and white phosphorus rocket pods on the sponsons. A pilot and rear seat observer/ aerial coordinator used the Bronco as a Forward Air Control aircraft to bring artillery and close air support aircraft to bear on ground targets. Peter B. Mersky

With the Vietnam War came another lax period in regulations, which allowed nose art to reappear. These TF-9J Cougars of H&MS-11 at Chu Lai, South Vietnam, 1967, were used for Fast Forward Air Control duties for about a year. Even with another squadron, H&MS-13, there were never more than around six to eight TF-9Js in-country. Here Capt. Peter L. Perkins stands next to his Cougar before a mission. Note the white phosphorus marker rocket pods. Peter B. Mersky

A YF-8A Crusader at the Naval Air Development Center, Johnsville, Pennsylvania, in 1965. John and Donna Campbell

This EC-47N of the 362nd Tactical Electronic Warfare Squadron, Da Nang, April 1972, was flown by Capt. John Winston. Gooney Birds were resurrected for several missions during the war, proving their utility and rugged nature. The shark mouth seemed to fit. Larry Davis

Carrying on the Flying Tigers tradition, an F-105D Thunderchief of the 23rd Tactical Fighter Wing heads for a target in Vietnam. Larry Davis

The 1st Infantry Division, the Big Red One, used OV-1C Mohawks with shark's teeth during their combat tour in Vietnam. The red division crest was usually painted on the center rudder.

29 December 1972—this 34th Squadron, 388th Tactical Fighter Wing F-4 Phantom II drop tank carried not only a shark mouth but a message to antiwar protestor Joan Baez who, when visiting Hanoi, accused American pilots of bombing the civilian airport at Gia Lam. *Harley Copic*

An early AH-1G Cobra in Vietnam, 1969, attached to A Troop, 1st Squadron, 7th Cavalry, US Army. Cespedes via Larry Davis

Huey gunships, January 1970, Vietnam, provide an excellent broad nose on which to paint teeth. Larry Davis

When the F-4E was deployed to Vietnam in 1968 with the 388th Tactical Fighter Wing, the pilots painted shark's teeth on their aircraft. The new internal-gun-equipped Phantom II seemed ideal for the marking, seen here on a 469th Squadron F-4E heading home from a mission. Logan

The LTV A-7D Corsair II was one of the last USAF aircraft types to see combat in Vietnam. When it arrived to fly with the 388th Wing, the shark's teeth fit in as a part of the unit's tradition, and they stayed for some time after the war ended, as seen here in December 1973. The 23rd Wing, carrying on the tradition of the Flying Tigers, had their A-7s painted with shark mouths before leaving for Vietnam.

An Air Force 20th Tactical Air Support Squadron OV-10A pulls in to its revetment at Udorn, Thailand, 29 June 1973. USAF via Larry Davis

F-105Gs of the 17th Wild Weasel Squadron at Korat, Thailand, February 1973, as the Vietnam War was coming to a close. Miller

Sharks Never Die

Though peace broke out in the 1970s, the shark did not disappear. Shark's teeth had become a military aviation tradition, never to be left dormant, as seen on this Canberra at the Royal Air Force base at Colerne, 8 March 1972. Alain Pelletier

Though the T-2 Buckeye advanced jet trainer did not carry anything more threatening than an instructor, shark's teeth found their way onto several assigned to VT-23 in 1982. The mouths didn't last in the highly regulated training environment. Peter B. Mersky

An A-7A Corsair II of VA-93 at Naval Air Facility Atsugi, Japan, April 1976. Jim Sullivan

The Fiat G.91 was well suited to shark's teeth, as seen on this R3 of LeKG 43 of the German Air Force, September 1975. Centurion Enterprises via Larry Davis

A Marine AH-1J SeaCobra lands on the amphibious transport dock USS Vancouver (LPD-2) off Palawan Island, 30 November 1974, during rehearsals for the joint US-Philippine amphibious exercise MABLEX-75. USN via David Ostrowski

Numerous surplus Sabres were bought by civilian companies in the 1970s and 1980s for drone conversion and military contract work. This one was painted with an effective shark mouth after being made operational.

The owner of this T-6F Texan got attention with his bright green paint and shark's teeth, 23 November 1974. Roger Besecker

An F-4N of VF-111 in June 1977 when attached to the USS Roosevelt. Larry Davis

This F-4C flew with the 122nd Tactical Fighter Wing, Fort Wayne, Indiana. Roth via Larry Davis

More than 5,000 Phantom IIs were built and shark's teeth showed up on many of them, in many styles. This late model F-4E had a particularly effective set of teeth.
Alain Pelletier

An F-4E of the 405th Tactical Fighter Wing, Clark Air Force Base, Philippines.

Royal Air Force Phantoms had some of the most imaginative shark mouths as can be seen on this FGR.2 of No. 56 Squadron, 23 July 1983. Alain Pelletier

South Korea, March 1986, an F-4E of the 497th Tactical Fighter Squadron during Team Spirit '86. USAF via Robert F. Dorr

A Mirage IIIRZ of the South African Air Force just after touchdown, 1990. SAAF

Though Flying Tigers Airlines was formed by former American Volunteer Group pilots after World War II, seldom did their transports carry the famous shark's teeth. This DC-8 was one of the few exceptions in the company's history before the line was sold to Federal Express. Ernest McDowell

This French T-6/Harvard restoration was painted in the markings of French forces in Algeria that were involved in supressing rebel uprisings. Alain Pelletier via Peter M. Bowers

An F-105F Thunderchief trainer of the Wild Weasel 35th Tactical Fighter Wing, George Air Force Base, California, 1980. The Weasel mission earned its shark's teeth as much as any in modern warfare.

Even pilots of very light aircraft, such as this Italian pusher, have to get in on the act. There is no denying the sinister look shark's teeth give even the most mundane flying machines. Peter M. Bowers

When the F-105Gs were transferred to the Georgia Air National Guard's 116th Tactical Fighter Wing, the Wild Weasels' shark mouths were given new life and a new style. Kirk Minert via Larry Davis

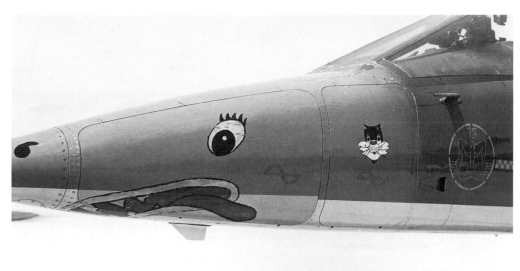

F-105Gs of the 116th Tactical Fighter Wing.
Peter Greve via Larry Davis

Some shark's teeth take on whimsical expressions. This French Air Force Jaguar was made to appear gasping for breath by the simple addition of a tongue hanging out. Alain Pelletier

*A B-52D of the 43rd Strategic Wing just
after delivery to Davis-Monthan Air Force
Base for storage.* Brian C. Rogers

Shark's teeth ready for action in an alert shelter. Larry Davis

This F-4E of the 131st Tactical Fighter Wing at Volk Field, Wisconsin, in October 1989 has two MiG kills painted on the splitter plate, a reflection of its Vietnam War combat record. Norris Graser

The "Remove Before Flight" red flags on this US Army T-34C at Pope Air Force Base, North Carolina, give the Turbo Mentor's shark mouth an added touch. Douglas A. Zalud

An F-4G Wild Weasel on the ramp at George Air Force Base, California, 14 June 1991. J.G. Handelman

The Alabama Air National Guard's 106th Tactical Reconnaissance Squadron flew shark RF-4Cs. Douglas A. Zalud

*A T-34C of TAW-5 at Naval Air Facility
Washington, DC, on 26 March 1985.* J.G.
Handelman

The Flying Tiger tradition lived on through subsequent aircraft of the 23rd Tactical Fighter Wing, such as this A-7D of the 74th Squadron at England Air Force Base, Louisiana, 3 June 1979. Norm Taylor

The A-10 was nicknamed the "Warthog," a near perfect ringer for the way it looks, so it was inevitable that someone would paint the animal's face on the nose. These A-10s of the 47th Tactical Fighter Squadron at Travis Field, Savannah, Georgia, in 1982 show the results. Norm Taylor

When the Sundowners converted to F-14 Tomcats, the sunburst tails and shark's teeth came along with them. Certainly VF-111 carried a colorful tradition for many years, one that has been hard to maintain in today's era of low-visibility gray paint schemes. H. Lapa/Roth

Miss Molly *was the CAG's (carrier-wing commander's) airplane on the USS Carl Vinson* with Carrier Air Wing 15. Few VF-111 aircraft have been more colorful *than this F-14A even the external fuel tanks had shark mouths.* J.G. Handelman/ Douglas A. Zalud

A closeup of the teeth on a 23rd Tactical Fighter Wing A-10. USAF

When the 23rd Tactical Fighter Wing transitioned to A-10 Thunderbolt IIs, the shark mouth remained a part of the tradition. On an airplane as mean looking as the A-10 the teeth enhance the business end of things. Norris Graser

The Warthog face ended up more subdued as arguments were made against camouflage disruption, but the idea is still there on this US Air Force Reserve A-10A. *Charles E. Mesker via Douglas A. Zalud*

When the Royal Air Force Tornado detachment began to fly combat out of Tabuk, Saudi Arabia, during Operation Desert Storm, all of the aircraft received shark's teeth and a generous dose of nose art. The mission symbols indicate this Tornado flew one mission with JP233, twenty-one with unguided 1,000lb bombs, and ten with 1,000lb laser-guided bombs. The name Gulf Killer was derived from the GK tail identification letters. *Alain Pelletier*

This Royal Air Force Puma helicopter saw extensive action in Desert Storm with a crew known as "The Flying Crazy Boys." Note the mission symbols on the door. Alain Pelletier

The Douglas Skywarrior served for a long time, finishing its years as a tanker and electronic warfare aircraft. This EA-3B of VQ-2 was still flying in the early 1990s. G. Turner

The commanding officer of No. 56 Squadron flew this Phantom FGR.2 from Wattisham, 6 August 1991. G. Turner

An F-16C Fighting Falcon of the 52nd Tactical Fighter Wing sports some mean teeth. Though camouflage colors continue to become more subdued and color is pulled off airplanes at an alarming rate, it seems shark's teeth will continue to be painted on aircraft. At times the teeth have had their color removed but the shark refuses to die . . . which will probably be the case as long as pilots fly airplanes. G. Turner

Index